This Audition Notebook

Belongs to:

· ·

DEDICATION

This book is dedicated to all the energetic and passionate Actors & Actresses out there who are working to get that role in your next performance!

Your are my inspiration for producing books and I'm so excited to be a part of helping you plan for your next audition!

I hope you fulfill all your goals, hopes and dreams with this Actors Audition Journal, notebook!

Action!

HOW TO USE THIS BOOK

The purpose of this book is to keep all of your Audition notes and information all in one place. It is a great way to record and keep track of your progress and will help keep you organized.

Here are some guidelines to follow so you can make the most out of using this book:

1. Production, Casting Director - Write the name of the show & who the casting director is.

2. Role - Jot down what role you are auditioning for.

3. Date, Time, Location - Record the date, time & location of your audition.

4. Sides, Headshot, Resume - Check the boxes to indicate you have given sides, headshot & resume.

5. Pieces Performed - Log which pieces you tried out for.

6. Behind The Table - Write name, contact info & feedback of auditioners.

7. How You Feel You Did - Rate how you think you did.

8. Notes, Blank Lined Ruled - Record any other important info you feel is necessary.

9. Call Back? Check the box if you get a call back.

Production _____   Date _____

Role _____   Time _____

Casting Director _____   Location _____

Sides ☐   Headshot ☐   Resume ☐

Pieces Performed

1. _____
2. _____
3. _____

Outfit _____

Behind the Table

Name	Contact Info	Feedback Received

Notes

_____

Feeling   Call Back? ☐

Production _____   Date _____

Role _____   Time _____

Casting Director _____   Location _____

Sides ☐   Headshot ☐   Resume ☐

Pieces Performed

1. _____
2. _____
3. _____

Outfit _____

Behind the Table

Name	Contact Info	Feedback Received

Notes

_____

Feeling   Call Back? ☐

Production _____   Date _____

Role _____   Time _____

Casting Director _____   Location _____

Sides ☐   Headshot ☐   Resume ☐

Pieces Performed

1. _____
2. _____
3. _____

Outfit _____

Behind the Table

Name	Contact Info	Feedback Received

Notes

Feeling   Call Back? ☐

Production _____   Date _____

Role _____   Time _____

Casting Director _____   Location _____

Sides ☐   Headshot ☐   Resume ☐

Pieces Performed

1. _____
2. _____
3. _____

Outfit _____

Behind the Table

Name	Contact Info	Feedback Received

Notes

Feeling    Call Back? ☐

Production _____   Date _____

Role _____   Time _____

Casting Director _____   Location _____

Sides ☐   Headshot ☐   Resume ☐

Pieces Performed

1. _____
2. _____
3. _____

Outfit _____

Behind the Table

Name	Contact Info	Feedback Received

Notes

_____

Feeling   Call Back? ☐

Production _____   Date _____

Role _____   Time _____

Casting Director _____   Location _____

Sides ☐   Headshot ☐   Resume ☐

Pieces Performed

1. _____
2. _____
3. _____

Outfit _____

Behind the Table

Name	Contact Info	Feedback Received

Notes

Feeling   Call Back? ☐

Production _____   Date _____

Role _____   Time _____

Casting Director _____   Location _____

Sides ☐   Headshot ☐   Resume ☐

Pieces Performed

1. _____
2. _____
3. _____

Outfit _____

Behind the Table

Name	Contact Info	Feedback Received

Notes

Feeling   😀   Call Back? ☐

Production _____   Date _____

Role _____   Time _____

Casting Director _____ Location _____

Sides ☐   Headshot ☐   Resume ☐

Pieces Performed

1. _____
2. _____
3. _____

Outfit _____

Behind the Table

Name	Contact Info	Feedback Received

Notes

Feeling    Call Back? ☐

Production _____   Date _____

Role _____   Time _____

Casting Director _____   Location _____

Sides ☐   Headshot ☐   Resume ☐

Pieces Performed

1. _____
2. _____
3. _____

Outfit _____

Behind the Table

Name	Contact Info	Feedback Received

Notes

Feeling   Call Back? ☐

Production _____   Date _____

Role _____   Time _____

Casting Director _____   Location _____

Sides ☐   Headshot ☐   Resume ☐

Pieces Performed

1. _____
2. _____
3. _____

Outfit _____

Behind the Table

Name	Contact Info	Feedback Received

Notes

[   ]

Feeling    Call Back? ☐

Production _____   Date _____

Role _____   Time _____

Casting Director _____   Location _____

Sides ☐   Headshot ☐   Resume ☐

Pieces Performed

1. _____
2. _____
3. _____

Outfit _____

Behind the Table

Name	Contact Info	Feedback Received

Notes

Feeling   😃   Call Back? ☐

Production _____   Date _____

Role _____   Time _____

Casting Director _____   Location _____

Sides ☐   Headshot ☐   Resume ☐

Pieces Performed

1. _____
2. _____
3. _____

Outfit _____

Behind the Table

Name	Contact Info	Feedback Received

Notes

Feeling    Call Back? ☐

Production _____   Date _____

Role _____   Time _____

Casting Director _____   Location _____

Sides ☐   Headshot ☐   Resume ☐

Pieces Performed

1. _____
2. _____
3. _____

Outfit _____

Behind the Table

Name	Contact Info	Feedback Received

Notes

Feeling   😃   Call Back? ☐

Production _____   Date _____

Role _____   Time _____

Casting Director _____   Location _____

Sides ☐   Headshot ☐   Resume ☐

Pieces Performed

1. _____
2. _____
3. _____

Outfit _____

Behind the Table

Name	Contact Info	Feedback Received

Notes

[   ]

Feeling   Call Back? ☐

Production _____   Date _____

Role _____   Time _____

Casting Director _____   Location _____

Sides ☐   Headshot ☐   Resume ☐

Pieces Performed

1. _____
2. _____
3. _____

Outfit _____

Behind the Table

Name	Contact Info	Feedback Received

Notes

Feeling   Call Back? ☐

Production _____ Date _____

Role _____ Time _____

Casting Director _____ Location _____

Sides ☐   Headshot ☐   Resume ☐

Pieces Performed

1. _____
2. _____
3. _____

Outfit _____

Behind the Table

Name	Contact Info	Feedback Received

Notes

Feeling   Call Back? ☐

Production _____   Date _____

Role _____   Time _____

Casting Director _____   Location _____

Sides ☐   Headshot ☐   Resume ☐

Pieces Performed

1. _____
2. _____
3. _____

Outfit _____

Behind the Table

Name	Contact Info	Feedback Received

Notes

Feeling   😄   Call Back? ☐

Production _____ Date _____

Role _____ Time _____

Casting Director _____ Location _____

Sides ☐   Headshot ☐   Resume ☐

Pieces Performed

1. _____
2. _____
3. _____

Outfit _____

Behind the Table

Name	Contact Info	Feedback Received

Notes

Feeling   Call Back? ☐

Production _____   Date _____

Role _____   Time _____

Casting Director _____   Location _____

Sides ☐   Headshot ☐   Resume ☐

Pieces Performed

1. _____
2. _____
3. _____

Outfit _____

Behind the Table

Name	Contact Info	Feedback Received

Notes

Feeling   Call Back? ☐

Production _____   Date _____

Role _____   Time _____

Casting Director _____   Location _____

Sides ☐   Headshot ☐   Resume ☐

Pieces Performed

1. _____
2. _____
3. _____

Outfit _____

Behind the Table

Name	Contact Info	Feedback Received

Notes

_____

Feeling   Call Back? ☐

Production _____   Date _____

Role _____   Time _____

Casting Director _____   Location _____

Sides ☐   Headshot ☐   Resume ☐

Pieces Performed

1. _____
2. _____
3. _____

Outfit _____

Behind the Table

Name	Contact Info	Feedback Received

Notes

_____

Feeling   Call Back? ☐

Production _____   Date _____

Role _____   Time _____

Casting Director _____   Location _____

Sides ☐   Headshot ☐   Resume ☐

Pieces Performed

1. _____
2. _____
3. _____

Outfit _____

Behind the Table

Name	Contact Info	Feedback Received

Notes

Feeling   Call Back? ☐

Production _____   Date _____

Role _____   Time _____

Casting Director _____   Location _____

Sides ☐   Headshot ☐   Resume ☐

Pieces Performed

1. _____
2. _____
3. _____

Outfit _____

Behind the Table

Name	Contact Info	Feedback Received

Notes

_____

Feeling   Call Back? ☐

Production _____   Date _____

Role _____   Time _____

Casting Director _____   Location _____

Sides ☐   Headshot ☐   Resume ☐

Pieces Performed

1. _____
2. _____
3. _____

Outfit _____

Behind the Table

Name	Contact Info	Feedback Received

Notes

_____

Feeling   Call Back? ☐

Production: _____ Date: _____

Role: _____ Time: _____

Casting Director: _____ Location: _____

Sides ☐   Headshot ☐   Resume ☐

Pieces Performed

1. _____
2. _____
3. _____

Outfit _____

Behind the Table

Name	Contact Info	Feedback Received

Notes

[   ]

Feeling   Call Back? ☐

Production _____   Date _____

Role _____   Time _____

Casting Director _____   Location _____

Sides ☐   Headshot ☐   Resume ☐

Pieces Performed

1. _____
2. _____
3. _____

Outfit _____

Behind the Table

Name	Contact Info	Feedback Received

Notes

_____

Feeling    Call Back? ☐

Production _____   Date _____

Role _____   Time _____

Casting Director _____   Location _____

Sides ☐   Headshot ☐   Resume ☐

Pieces Performed

1. _____
2. _____
3. _____

Outfit _____

Behind the Table

Name	Contact Info	Feedback Received

Notes

_____

Feeling   Call Back? ☐

Production _____   Date _____

Role _____   Time _____

Casting Director _____   Location _____

Sides ☐   Headshot ☐   Resume ☐

Pieces Performed

1. _____
2. _____
3. _____

Outfit _____

Behind the Table

Name	Contact Info	Feedback Received

Notes

Feeling   Call Back? ☐

Production _____ Date _____

Role _____ Time _____

Casting Director _____ Location _____

Sides ☐   Headshot ☐   Resume ☐

Pieces Performed

1. _____
2. _____
3. _____

Outfit _____

Behind the Table

Name	Contact Info	Feedback Received

Notes

_____

Feeling   Call Back? ☐

Production _____ Date _____

Role _____ Time _____

Casting Director _____ Location _____

Sides ☐   Headshot ☐   Resume ☐

Pieces Performed

1. _____
2. _____
3. _____

Outfit _____

Behind the Table

Name	Contact Info	Feedback Received

Notes

Feeling 😐 😴 😮 🙂 😃   Call Back? ☐

Production _____   Date _____

Role _____   Time _____

Casting Director _____   Location _____

Sides ☐   Headshot ☐   Resume ☐

Pieces Performed

1. _____
2. _____
3. _____

Outfit _____

Behind the Table

Name	Contact Info	Feedback Received

Notes

_____

Feeling   Call Back? ☐

Production _____ Date _____

Role _____ Time _____

Casting Director _____ Location _____

Sides ☐ Headshot ☐ Resume ☐

Pieces Performed

1. _____
2. _____
3. _____

Outfit _____

Behind the Table

Name	Contact Info	Feedback Received

Notes

Feeling 😐 😪 😲 🙂 😃   Call Back? ☐

Production _____   Date _____

Role _____   Time _____

Casting Director _____ Location _____

Sides ☐   Headshot ☐   Resume ☐

Pieces Performed

1. _____
2. _____
3. _____

Outfit _____

Behind the Table

Name	Contact Info	Feedback Received

Notes

Feeling   Call Back? ☐

Production _____   Date _____

Role _____   Time _____

Casting Director _____   Location _____

Sides ☐   Headshot ☐   Resume ☐

Pieces Performed

1. _____
2. _____
3. _____

Outfit _____

Behind the Table

Name	Contact Info	Feedback Received

Notes

Feeling   Call Back? ☐

Production _____   Date _____

Role _____   Time _____

Casting Director _____   Location _____

Sides ☐   Headshot ☐   Resume ☐

Pieces Performed

1. _____
2. _____
3. _____

Outfit _____

Behind the Table

Name	Contact Info	Feedback Received

Notes

Feeling   Call Back? ☐

Production _____   Date _____

Role _____   Time _____

Casting Director _____   Location _____

Sides ☐   Headshot ☐   Resume ☐

Pieces Performed

1. _____
2. _____
3. _____

Outfit _____

Behind the Table

Name	Contact Info	Feedback Received

Notes

Feeling   Call Back? ☐

Production _____   Date _____

Role _____   Time _____

Casting Director _____   Location _____

Sides ☐   Headshot ☐   Resume ☐

Pieces Performed

1. _____
2. _____
3. _____

Outfit _____

Behind the Table

Name	Contact Info	Feedback Received

Notes

[   ]

Feeling   Call Back? ☐

Production _____   Date _____

Role _____   Time _____

Casting Director _____   Location _____

Sides ☐   Headshot ☐   Resume ☐

Pieces Performed

1. _____
2. _____
3. _____

Outfit _____

Behind the Table

Name	Contact Info	Feedback Received

Notes

Feeling    Call Back? ☐

Production _____   Date _____

Role _____   Time _____

Casting Director _____   Location _____

Sides ☐   Headshot ☐   Resume ☐

Pieces Performed

1. _____
2. _____
3. _____

Outfit _____

Behind the Table

Name	Contact Info	Feedback Received

Notes

Feeling   Call Back? ☐

Production _____   Date _____

Role _____   Time _____

Casting Director _____   Location _____

Sides ☐   Headshot ☐   Resume ☐

Pieces Performed

1. _____
2. _____
3. _____

Outfit _____

Behind the Table

Name	Contact Info	Feedback Received

Notes

Feeling   Call Back? ☐

Production _____   Date _____

Role _____   Time _____

Casting Director _____   Location _____

Sides ☐   Headshot ☐   Resume ☐

Pieces Performed

1. _____
2. _____
3. _____

Outfit _____

Behind the Table

Name	Contact Info	Feedback Received

Notes

Feeling   😀   Call Back? ☐

Production _____   Date _____

Role _____   Time _____

Casting Director _____   Location _____

Sides ☐   Headshot ☐   Resume ☐

Pieces Performed

1. _____
2. _____
3. _____

Outfit _____

Behind the Table

Name	Contact Info	Feedback Received

Notes

Feeling   Call Back? ☐

Production _____ Date _____

Role _____ Time _____

Casting Director _____ Location _____

Sides ☐   Headshot ☐   Resume ☐

Pieces Performed

1. _____
2. _____
3. _____

Outfit _____

Behind the Table

Name	Contact Info	Feedback Received

Notes

Feeling   Call Back? ☐

Production _____   Date _____

Role _____   Time _____

Casting Director _____   Location _____

Sides ☐   Headshot ☐   Resume ☐

Pieces Performed

1. _____
2. _____
3. _____

Outfit _____

Behind the Table

Name	Contact Info	Feedback Received

Notes

Feeling    Call Back? ☐

Production _____   Date _____

Role _____   Time _____

Casting Director _____   Location _____

Sides ☐   Headshot ☐   Resume ☐

Pieces Performed

1. _____
2. _____
3. _____

Outfit _____

Behind the Table

Name	Contact Info	Feedback Received

Notes

_____

Feeling   Call Back? ☐

Production _____   Date _____

Role _____   Time _____

Casting Director _____   Location _____

Sides ☐   Headshot ☐   Resume ☐

Pieces Performed

1. _____
2. _____
3. _____

Outfit _____

Behind the Table

Name	Contact Info	Feedback Received

Notes

Feeling   Call Back? ☐

Production _____   Date _____

Role _____   Time _____

Casting Director _____   Location _____

Sides ☐   Headshot ☐   Resume ☐

Pieces Performed

1. _____
2. _____
3. _____

Outfit _____

Behind the Table

Name	Contact Info	Feedback Received

Notes

_____

Feeling   Call Back? ☐

Production	_____	Date	_____
Role	_____	Time	_____
Casting Director	_____	Location	_____

Sides ☐   Headshot ☐   Resume ☐

Pieces Performed

1. _____
2. _____
3. _____

Outfit _____

Behind the Table

Name	Contact Info	Feedback Received

Notes

[   ]

Feeling   Call Back? ☐

Production _____   Date _____

Role _____   Time _____

Casting Director _____ Location _____

Sides ☐   Headshot ☐   Resume ☐

Pieces Performed

1. _____
2. _____
3. _____

Outfit _____

Behind the Table

Name	Contact Info	Feedback Received

Notes

Feeling   Call Back? ☐

Production _____   Date _____

Role _____   Time _____

Casting Director _____ Location _____

Sides ☐   Headshot ☐   Resume ☐

Pieces Performed

1. _____
2. _____
3. _____

Outfit _____

Behind the Table

Name	Contact Info	Feedback Received

Notes

Feeling   Call Back? ☐

Production _____   Date _____

Role _____   Time _____

Casting Director _____   Location _____

Sides ☐   Headshot ☐   Resume ☐

Pieces Performed

1. _____
2. _____
3. _____

Outfit _____

Behind the Table

Name	Contact Info	Feedback Received

Notes

Feeling   Call Back? ☐

Production _____   Date _____

Role _____   Time _____

Casting Director _____   Location _____

Sides ☐   Headshot ☐   Resume ☐

Pieces Performed

1. _____
2. _____
3. _____

Outfit _____

Behind the Table

Name	Contact Info	Feedback Received

Notes

Feeling   Call Back? ☐

Production _____   Date _____

Role _____   Time _____

Casting Director _____   Location _____

Sides ☐   Headshot ☐   Resume ☐

Pieces Performed

1. _____
2. _____
3. _____

Outfit _____

Behind the Table

Name	Contact Info	Feedback Received

Notes

Feeling   Call Back? ☐

Production _____   Date _____

Role _____   Time _____

Casting Director _____   Location _____

Sides ☐   Headshot ☐   Resume ☐

Pieces Performed

1. _____
2. _____
3. _____

Outfit _____

Behind the Table

Name	Contact Info	Feedback Received

Notes

Feeling    Call Back? ☐

Production _____   Date _____

Role _____   Time _____

Casting Director _____   Location _____

Sides ☐   Headshot ☐   Resume ☐

Pieces Performed

1. _____
2. _____
3. _____

Outfit _____

Behind the Table

Name	Contact Info	Feedback Received

Notes

[   ]

Feeling   Call Back? ☐

Production _____   Date _____

Role _____   Time _____

Casting Director _____   Location _____

Sides ☐   Headshot ☐   Resume ☐

Pieces Performed

1. _____
2. _____
3. _____

Outfit _____

Behind the Table

Name	Contact Info	Feedback Received

Notes

Feeling   Call Back? ☐

Production _____   Date _____

Role _____   Time _____

Casting Director _____   Location _____

Sides ☐   Headshot ☐   Resume ☐

Pieces Performed

1. _____
2. _____
3. _____

Outfit _____

Behind the Table

Name	Contact Info	Feedback Received

Notes

Feeling   Call Back? ☐

Production _____   Date _____

Role _____   Time _____

Casting Director _____   Location _____

Sides ☐   Headshot ☐   Resume ☐

Pieces Performed

1. _____
2. _____
3. _____

Outfit _____

Behind the Table

Name	Contact Info	Feedback Received

Notes

Feeling   Call Back? ☐

Production _____   Date _____

Role _____   Time _____

Casting Director _____   Location _____

Sides ☐   Headshot ☐   Resume ☐

Pieces Performed

1. _____
2. _____
3. _____

Outfit _____

Behind the Table

Name	Contact Info	Feedback Received

Notes

Feeling   😃   Call Back? ☐

Production _____   Date _____

Role _____   Time _____

Casting Director _____   Location _____

Sides ☐   Headshot ☐   Resume ☐

Pieces Performed

1. _____
2. _____
3. _____

Outfit _____

Behind the Table

Name	Contact Info	Feedback Received

Notes

_____

Feeling   Call Back? ☐

Production _____   Date _____

Role _____   Time _____

Casting Director _____   Location _____

Sides ☐   Headshot ☐   Resume ☐

Pieces Performed

1. _____
2. _____
3. _____

Outfit _____

Behind the Table

Name	Contact Info	Feedback Received

Notes

Feeling   Call Back? ☐

Production _____   Date _____

Role _____   Time _____

Casting Director _____   Location _____

Sides ☐   Headshot ☐   Resume ☐

Pieces Performed

1. _____
2. _____
3. _____

Outfit _____

Behind the Table

Name	Contact Info	Feedback Received

Notes

Feeling    Call Back? ☐

Production _____   Date _____

Role _____   Time _____

Casting Director _____ Location _____

Sides ☐   Headshot ☐   Resume ☐

Pieces Performed

1. _____
2. _____
3. _____

Outfit _____

Behind the Table

Name	Contact Info	Feedback Received

Notes

_____

Feeling   Call Back? ☐

Production _____   Date _____

Role _____   Time _____

Casting Director _____   Location _____

Sides ☐   Headshot ☐   Resume ☐

Pieces Performed

1. _____
2. _____
3. _____

Outfit _____

Behind the Table

Name	Contact Info	Feedback Received

Notes

_____

Feeling   Call Back? ☐

Production _____   Date _____

Role _____   Time _____

Casting Director _____   Location _____

Sides ☐   Headshot ☐   Resume ☐

Pieces Performed

1. _____
2. _____
3. _____

Outfit _____

Behind the Table

Name	Contact Info	Feedback Received

Notes

Feeling   Call Back? ☐

Production _____   Date _____

Role _____   Time _____

Casting Director _____   Location _____

Sides ☐   Headshot ☐   Resume ☐

Pieces Performed

1. _____
2. _____
3. _____

Outfit _____

Behind the Table

Name	Contact Info	Feedback Received

Notes

Feeling   Call Back? ☐

Production _____   Date _____

Role _____   Time _____

Casting Director _____ Location _____

Sides ☐   Headshot ☐   Resume ☐

Pieces Performed

1. _____
2. _____
3. _____

Outfit _____

Behind the Table

Name	Contact Info	Feedback Received

Notes

_____

Feeling   Call Back? ☐

Production _____   Date _____

Role _____   Time _____

Casting Director _____   Location _____

Sides ☐   Headshot ☐   Resume ☐

Pieces Performed

1. _____
2. _____
3. _____

Outfit _____

Behind the Table

Name	Contact Info	Feedback Received

Notes

Feeling   Call Back? ☐

Production _____   Date _____

Role _____   Time _____

Casting Director _____   Location _____

Sides [ ]   Headshot [ ]   Resume [ ]

Pieces Performed

1. _____
2. _____
3. _____

Outfit _____

Behind the Table

Name	Contact Info	Feedback Received

Notes

Feeling   Call Back? [ ]

Production _____   Date _____

Role _____   Time _____

Casting Director _____   Location _____

Sides ☐   Headshot ☐   Resume ☐

Pieces Performed

1. _____
2. _____
3. _____

Outfit _____

Behind the Table

Name	Contact Info	Feedback Received

Notes

Feeling    Call Back? ☐

Production _____   Date _____

Role _____   Time _____

Casting Director _____   Location _____

Sides ☐   Headshot ☐   Resume ☐

Pieces Performed

1. _____
2. _____
3. _____

Outfit _____

Behind the Table

Name	Contact Info	Feedback Received

Notes

Feeling   Call Back? ☐

Production _____   Date _____

Role _____   Time _____

Casting Director _____   Location _____

Sides ☐   Headshot ☐   Resume ☐

Pieces Performed

1. _____
2. _____
3. _____

Outfit _____

Behind the Table

Name	Contact Info	Feedback Received

Notes

[   ]

Feeling   Call Back? ☐

Production _____   Date _____

Role _____   Time _____

Casting Director _____   Location _____

Sides ☐   Headshot ☐   Resume ☐

Pieces Performed

1. _____
2. _____
3. _____

Outfit _____

Behind the Table

Name	Contact Info	Feedback Received

Notes

Feeling   😄   Call Back? ☐

Production _____ Date _____

Role _____ Time _____

Casting Director _____ Location _____

Sides ☐   Headshot ☐   Resume ☐

Pieces Performed

1. _____
2. _____
3. _____

Outfit _____

Behind the Table

Name	Contact Info	Feedback Received

Notes

Feeling    Call Back? ☐

Production _____   Date _____

Role _____   Time _____

Casting Director _____ Location _____

Sides ☐   Headshot ☐   Resume ☐

Pieces Performed

1. _____
2. _____
3. _____

Outfit _____

Behind the Table

Name	Contact Info	Feedback Received

Notes

[   ]

Feeling   Call Back? ☐

Production _____   Date _____

Role _____   Time _____

Casting Director _____   Location _____

Sides ☐   Headshot ☐   Resume ☐

Pieces Performed

1. _____
2. _____
3. _____

Outfit _____

Behind the Table

Name	Contact Info	Feedback Received

Notes

_____
_____
_____
_____

Feeling    Call Back? ☐

Production _____ Date _____

Role _____ Time _____

Casting Director _____ Location _____

Sides ☐   Headshot ☐   Resume ☐

Pieces Performed

1. _____
2. _____
3. _____

Outfit _____

Behind the Table

Name	Contact Info	Feedback Received

Notes

Feeling   Call Back? ☐

Production _____   Date _____

Role _____   Time _____

Casting Director _____   Location _____

Sides ☐   Headshot ☐   Resume ☐

Pieces Performed

1. _____
2. _____
3. _____

Outfit _____

Behind the Table

Name	Contact Info	Feedback Received

Notes

Feeling    Call Back? ☐

Production _____   Date _____

Role _____   Time _____

Casting Director _____   Location _____

Sides ☐   Headshot ☐   Resume ☐

Pieces Performed

1. _____
2. _____
3. _____

Outfit _____

Behind the Table

Name	Contact Info	Feedback Received

Notes

Feeling   😃   Call Back? ☐

Production _____   Date _____

Role _____   Time _____

Casting Director _____   Location _____

Sides ☐   Headshot ☐   Resume ☐

Pieces Performed

1. _____
2. _____
3. _____

Outfit _____

Behind the Table

Name	Contact Info	Feedback Received

Notes

_____

Feeling   Call Back? ☐

Production _____ Date _____

Role _____ Time _____

Casting Director _____ Location _____

Sides ☐   Headshot ☐   Resume ☐

Pieces Performed

1. _____
2. _____
3. _____

Outfit _____

Behind the Table

Name	Contact Info	Feedback Received

Notes

_____

Feeling   Call Back? ☐

Production _____   Date _____

Role _____   Time _____

Casting Director _____   Location _____

Sides ☐   Headshot ☐   Resume ☐

Pieces Performed

1. _____
2. _____
3. _____

Outfit _____

Behind the Table

Name	Contact Info	Feedback Received

Notes

Feeling   Call Back? ☐

Production _____   Date _____

Role _____   Time _____

Casting Director _____   Location _____

Sides ☐   Headshot ☐   Resume ☐

Pieces Performed

1. _____
2. _____
3. _____

Outfit _____

Behind the Table

Name	Contact Info	Feedback Received

Notes

Feeling   Call Back? ☐

Production _____   Date _____

Role _____   Time _____

Casting Director _____   Location _____

Sides ☐   Headshot ☐   Resume ☐

Pieces Performed

1. _____
2. _____
3. _____

Outfit _____

Behind the Table

Name	Contact Info	Feedback Received

Notes

Feeling   Call Back? ☐

Production _____   Date _____

Role _____   Time _____

Casting Director _____   Location _____

Sides ☐   Headshot ☐   Resume ☐

Pieces Performed

1. _____
2. _____
3. _____

Outfit _____

Behind the Table

Name	Contact Info	Feedback Received

Notes

Feeling   Call Back? ☐

Production _____   Date _____

Role _____   Time _____

Casting Director _____ Location _____

Sides ☐   Headshot ☐   Resume ☐

Pieces Performed

1. _____
2. _____
3. _____

Outfit _____

Behind the Table

Name	Contact Info	Feedback Received

Notes

Feeling   Call Back? ☐

Production _____   Date _____

Role _____   Time _____

Casting Director _____   Location _____

Sides ☐   Headshot ☐   Resume ☐

Pieces Performed

1. _____
2. _____
3. _____

Outfit _____

Behind the Table

Name	Contact Info	Feedback Received

Notes

_____

Feeling   Call Back? ☐

Production _____   Date _____

Role _____   Time _____

Casting Director _____   Location _____

Sides ☐   Headshot ☐   Resume ☐

Pieces Performed

1. _____

2. _____

3. _____

Outfit _____

Behind the Table

Name	Contact Info	Feedback Received

Notes

Feeling    Call Back? ☐

Production _____   Date _____

Role _____   Time _____

Casting Director _____   Location _____

Sides ☐   Headshot ☐   Resume ☐

Pieces Performed

1. _____
2. _____
3. _____

Outfit _____

Behind the Table

Name	Contact Info	Feedback Received

Notes

_____

Feeling   Call Back? ☐

Production _____   Date _____

Role _____   Time _____

Casting Director _____   Location _____

Sides ☐   Headshot ☐   Resume ☐

Pieces Performed

1. _____
2. _____
3. _____

Outfit _____

Behind the Table

Name	Contact Info	Feedback Received

Notes

Feeling   Call Back? ☐

Production _____   Date _____

Role _____   Time _____

Casting Director _____ Location _____

Sides ☐   Headshot ☐   Resume ☐

Pieces Performed

1. _____
2. _____
3. _____

Outfit _____

Behind the Table

Name	Contact Info	Feedback Received

Notes

Feeling   Call Back? ☐

Production _____   Date _____

Role _____   Time _____

Casting Director _____   Location _____

Sides ☐   Headshot ☐   Resume ☐

Pieces Performed

1. _____
2. _____
3. _____

Outfit _____

Behind the Table

Name	Contact Info	Feedback Received

Notes

Feeling   Call Back? ☐

Production _____   Date _____

Role _____   Time _____

Casting Director _____   Location _____

Sides ☐   Headshot ☐   Resume ☐

Pieces Performed

1. _____
2. _____
3. _____

Outfit _____

Behind the Table

Name	Contact Info	Feedback Received

Notes

Feeling   Call Back? ☐

Production _____   Date _____

Role _____   Time _____

Casting Director _____   Location _____

Sides ☐   Headshot ☐   Resume ☐

Pieces Performed

1. _____
2. _____
3. _____

Outfit _____

Behind the Table

Name	Contact Info	Feedback Received

Notes

_____

Feeling   Call Back? ☐

Production _____ Date _____

Role _____ Time _____

Casting Director _____ Location _____

Sides ☐   Headshot ☐   Resume ☐

Pieces Performed

1. _____
2. _____
3. _____

Outfit _____

Behind the Table

Name	Contact Info	Feedback Received

Notes

_____

Feeling   Call Back? ☐

Production _____   Date _____

Role _____   Time _____

Casting Director _____   Location _____

Sides ☐   Headshot ☐   Resume ☐

Pieces Performed

1. _____
2. _____
3. _____

Outfit _____

Behind the Table

Name	Contact Info	Feedback Received

Notes

Feeling   Call Back? ☐

Production _____   Date _____

Role _____   Time _____

Casting Director _____   Location _____

Sides ☐   Headshot ☐   Resume ☐

Pieces Performed

1. _____
2. _____
3. _____

Outfit _____

Behind the Table

Name	Contact Info	Feedback Received

Notes

[   ]

Feeling 😐 😙 😯 🙂 😀   Call Back? ☐

Production _____   Date _____

Role _____   Time _____

Casting Director _____   Location _____

Sides ☐   Headshot ☐   Resume ☐

Pieces Performed

1. _____
2. _____
3. _____

Outfit _____

Behind the Table

Name	Contact Info	Feedback Received

Notes

Feeling   Call Back? ☐

Production _____   Date _____

Role _____   Time _____

Casting Director _____   Location _____

Sides ☐   Headshot ☐   Resume ☐

Pieces Performed

1. _____
2. _____
3. _____

Outfit _____

Behind the Table

Name	Contact Info	Feedback Received

Notes

_____

Feeling   😀   Call Back? ☐

Production _____ Date _____

Role _____ Time _____

Casting Director _____ Location _____

Sides ☐   Headshot ☐   Resume ☐

Pieces Performed

1. _____
2. _____
3. _____

Outfit _____

Behind the Table

Name	Contact Info	Feedback Received

Notes

_____

Feeling   Call Back? ☐

Production _____ Date _____

Role _____ Time _____

Casting Director _____ Location _____

Sides ☐   Headshot ☐   Resume ☐

Pieces Performed

1. _____
2. _____
3. _____

Outfit _____

Behind the Table

Name	Contact Info	Feedback Received

Notes

Feeling   Call Back? ☐

Production _____   Date _____

Role _____   Time _____

Casting Director _____   Location _____

Sides ☐   Headshot ☐   Resume ☐

Pieces Performed

1. _____
2. _____
3. _____

Outfit _____

Behind the Table

Name	Contact Info	Feedback Received

Notes

_____
_____
_____
_____

Feeling   Call Back? ☐

Production _____   Date _____

Role _____   Time _____

Casting Director _____   Location _____

Sides ☐   Headshot ☐   Resume ☐

Pieces Performed

1. _____
2. _____
3. _____

Outfit _____

Behind the Table

Name	Contact Info	Feedback Received

Notes

Feeling   Call Back? ☐

Production _____   Date _____

Role _____   Time _____

Casting Director _____   Location _____

Sides ☐   Headshot ☐   Resume ☐

Pieces Performed

1. _____
2. _____
3. _____

Outfit _____

Behind the Table

Name	Contact Info	Feedback Received

Notes

_____

Feeling   Call Back? ☐

Production _____   Date _____

Role _____   Time _____

Casting Director _____   Location _____

Sides ☐   Headshot ☐   Resume ☐

Pieces Performed

1. _____
2. _____
3. _____

Outfit _____

Behind the Table

Name	Contact Info	Feedback Received

Notes

_____

Feeling   Call Back? ☐